WHALING DAYS

BY CAROL CARRICK
WOODCUTS BY DAVID FRAMPTON

CLARION BOOKS • NEW YORK

This book is dedicated to the Greenpeace Whale Campaign
in their efforts to save the whales.

—Carol Carrick

This book is dedicated to Mr. Smalley—a real American harpooneer.

—David Frampton

My thanks to the people of the Wampanoag tribe
of Gay Head, Massachusetts.

—D F

Clarion Books
a Houghton Mifflin Company imprint
215 Park Avenue South, New York, NY 10003
Text copyright © 1993 by Carol Carrick
Illustrations copyright © 1993 by David Frampton
All rights reserved.
For information about permission to reproduce selections
from this book, write to Permissions,
Houghton Mifflin Company, 215 Park Avenue South,
New York, NY 10003.
For information about this and other Houghton Mifflin trade
and reference books and multimedia products, visit
The Bookstore at Houghton Mifflin on the World Wide Web
at (http://www.hmco.com/trade/).

BVG 10 9 8 7 6 5 4 3

Library of Congress Cataloging-in-Publication Data
Carrick, Carol.
   Whaling days / by Carol Carrick ; illustrated by David Frampton.
     p.   cm.
   Summary: Surveys the whaling industry, ranging from hunting in
colonial America to modern whaling regulations and conservation efforts.
   ISBN 0-395-50948-3   PA ISBN 0-395-76480-7
   1. Whaling—Juvenile literature.   2. Whaling—United States—
Juvenile literature.   3. Whales—Juvenile literature.   [1. Whaling.
2. Whales.]   I. Frampton, David, ill.   II. Title.   91-22483
SH381.5.C37   1992   CIP
639.2'8—dc20   AC

Since ancient times, people have stood in awe of the whale, the largest creature that ever lived. They have also made use of the whale to help provide them with the necessities of life.

Whales found stranded on the beach were used for food. Sometimes the smaller species were hunted from boats. Shouting and making a great deal of noise, people drove the whales into shallow water, where they could stab them with many spears or arrows.

By the twelfth century, Basque fishermen were selling whale meat in Europe. But it wasn't until the seventeenth century, when whale oil was in great demand in Europe, that whaling became an industry. At that time the Dutch and the English began competing for whales in the northern seas.

Whales have a thick layer of fat under their skin, called blubber, that keeps them warm. Dutch and English whale hunters cooked oil out of this blubber and shipped it back to Europe in barrels. There it was burned in lamps and used for making soap and candles.

BLUE

HUMPBACK

SPERM

RIGHT

When the Pilgrims came to America in 1620, Cape Cod Bay was full of whales. The early settlers were not whalemen, and at first they killed only beached whales. Then, by watching the Native Americans, the settlers learned how to hunt whales.

When a whale was sighted offshore, the Native Americans paddled out in their canoes to stab it with harpoons. A chunk of wood called a drogue was

attached to the end of a strong vine on each harpoon. The drogues slowed down the escaping whale so that the hunters could follow and kill it with their lances.

After the whale died from loss of blood, the hunters cut a hole in its jaw, fastened a strong line through it, and towed the floating carcass to shore, where they cut it up for food. When the colonists began to hunt whales, skilled Native Americans made up half of the whaling crews.

Around 1645, settlers from Southampton on New York's Long Island began to hunt whales along the coast. The crews sailed for two or three weeks at a time, camping on the beach at night.

Once they killed a whale, the crewmen cut its blubber into chunks and hauled them aboard their boats. Onshore, the chunks were cooked in big iron try-pots, releasing valuable oil by the barrelful. This process was called trying-out.

As more settlers came to America, whaling spread with them to Connecticut, Rhode Island, and the island of Martha's Vineyard.

In 1690, settlers on Nantucket Island, Massachusetts, brought renowned whaler Ichabod Paddock from Cape Cod to teach them whaling. Paddock divided the ocean side of the island into four sections. Each section had a lookout post so the islanders could scan the horizon for whales.

A whale has to come to the surface to breathe air through its blowhole. Its spout of misty breath can be seen from a mile away. When the lookout saw a spout, he shouted "Whale off!" and hoisted a signal flag. Then all the Nantucket crews launched their boats from the beach.

Early whalers hunted the right whale, a good source of oil and whalebone. It was gentle, it swam close to shore, and it floated after it was killed, so it was easy to tow. For these reasons, whalers considered it the "right" one to catch.

Fifty-foot, fifty-ton right whales have no teeth. They strain their food out of seawater by forcing the water through baleen, bony slats in the upper jaw. Whalebone, another name for baleen, is both lightweight and strong. This made it useful for many things—fishing rods, carriage springs, umbrellas, fans, hoops, and ladies' corsets.

Pursued by whalers of many nations, right whales became scarce. By the early 1700s, a hundred years after offshore whaling began in the American colonies, the Atlantic right whales had almost disappeared.

Meanwhile, in 1712, a Nantucket ship first reported killing a different whale—the sperm whale. It is a hard-fighting, fifty-five-foot whale with teeth. The sperm whale prowls the deep ocean, living on octopus and giant squid. It can swallow chunks of food half the size of a twenty-seven-foot whaleboat.

Inside the sperm whale's enormous head is a hollow filled with a pure, clear oil, called spermaceti. This oil gave the whale its name. When exposed to the air, spermaceti hardened into a waxy substance that was prized for making candles.

When a right whale was harpooned it was allowed to run, pulling the drogues, till it tired. But a sperm whale was faster. In order to keep the whale in sight, whalers attached the harpoon line to the boat itself so the fleeing whale pulled the boat after it.

As more whalers successfully pursued sperm whales, whaling became an important business in the American colonies. By the mid-1700s, New England was producing more oil and whalebone than it needed. These products were sent back to England, which forbade the colonies to send them to any other

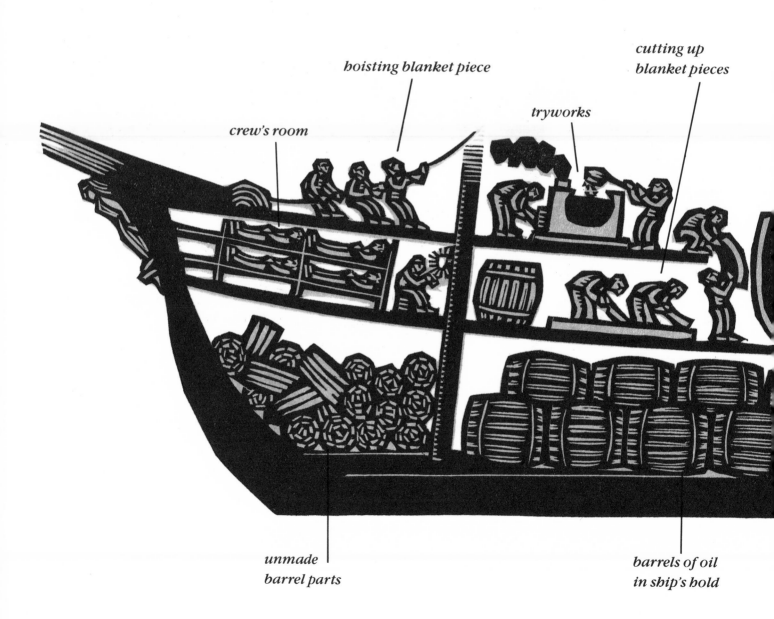

crew's room

hoisting blanket piece

cutting up
blanket pieces

tryworks

unmade
barrel parts

barrels of oil
in ship's hold

country. At the same time, the British taxed these imports to support their own failing whale industry.

The American whaling fleet of 360 ships was nearly destroyed by the British during the Revolution and the War of 1812. Sailors were often kidnapped and forced to serve in the English navy. But the United States was growing, and needed even more oil and candles. Between 1825 and 1860 the whaling fleet rose to 735 ships. New Bedford, Massachusetts, with its deep harbor, became the whaling capital of the world.

Sperm whales grew scarce in the Atlantic, so bigger ships were built to sail past the tips of Africa and South America. Larger crews were needed to man these ships and to hunt down whales in the Indian, Pacific, and Arctic oceans. During the three or four years it might take to fill all the barrels in a ship's hold, the whalemen lived on board ship.

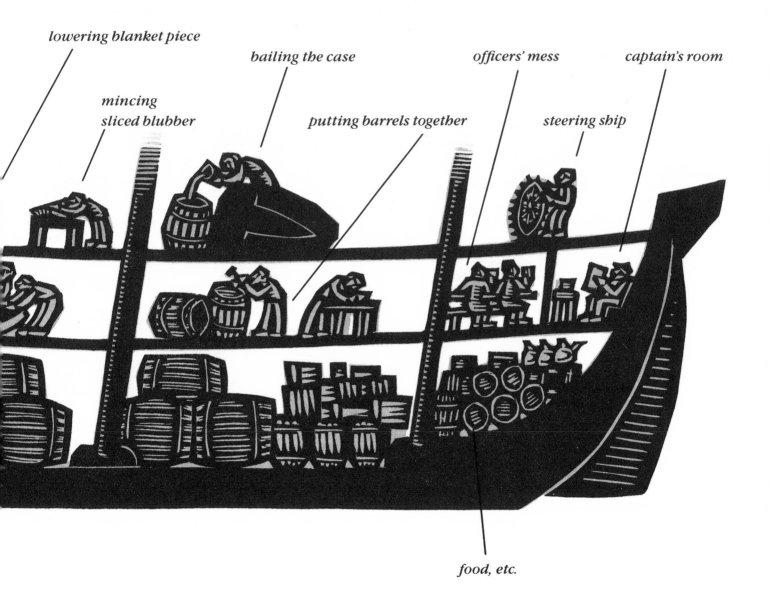

lowering blanket piece

mincing sliced blubber

bailing the case

putting barrels together

officers' mess

steering ship

captain's room

food, etc.

Life was hard on these long trips. The captain was master, and men were severely punished if they disobeyed his orders. Many sailors drowned, or died in accidents or from disease. Some froze to death; others were killed by whales.

The captain and from one to four mates each had his own cabin. Little room was left for the crew of twenty-five to forty-five men. Those with special jobs like barrel maker, carpenter, sail maker, blacksmith, and cook slept in bunkrooms. The rest crowded into one dark room under the forward deck. They slept in double, sometimes triple, rows of short, narrow bunks.

To leave space for the barrels of precious whale oil, there were only enough bunks for half the crew. So half of the men worked—washing decks, setting sails, sharpening tools, and steering—while the other half slept.

Each man kept his possessions in a small chest, which was also used as a seat. Light came from a single lantern. The only air in the close, smelly crew's room came through the hatch door overhead, which had to be closed in foul weather. There were no toilets, and the sailors used salty seawater for washing.

The officers ate together in the main cabin, and were served by a cabin boy. The crew ate on deck, and their food was usually the same every day—salted meat, beans, and a dry biscuit called hardtack. For a special treat, the cook might make a dessert from dried apples and raisins. On long voyages, the bread got moldy, the meat spoiled, and even the drinking water turned bad.

Either the captain or his first mate kept a log—a record of the voyage and the whales that were sighted, lost, or killed.

Sometimes the sailors would not sight a whale for many weeks. To pass the time, they made scrimshaw, carvings from a sperm whale's tooth or from a piece of its lower jaw. They shaped the tooth or bone into presents for their loved ones—clothespins, knitting needles, pretty boxes—and decorated the gifts by scratching pictures on their polished surfaces.

Once in a while two ships met at sea and held a gam. This was a sociable time, lasting a day or so, when the captain and his crew could visit the men on the other ship. A gam gave the sailors a chance to exchange news and send letters back with a ship that was going home.

Each of the hands took his turn in the crow's nest, a perch high in the tallest mast, to watch for whales. When he spied a whale in the distance, the man sang out, "Blows! She blows!"

The crew scrambled to their places. Three or four small boats were let down over the side. Each one held oars, a mast and sail, two tubs containing hundreds of feet of rope, drogues, and a bucket to bail out the boat. There were also harpoons, lances, and fresh water and a compass in case the boat was separated from the ship.

The whalemen leaped in. Five men rowed each boat, pulling hard against their oars, in a race that might take hours. The captain or one of his mates stood facing forward to steer with his long oar.

At last they could hear the whale breathe—feel its breath on their backs. But the men never turned, never broke their stroke.

"Steady." The mate spoke softly. He did not want to alarm the whale.

The harpooneer put down his oar and rose to his feet in the bow. Carefully, he aimed a harpoon, then hurtled it deep into the whale's side.

"Hit him again!" called the mate. "Hit him with all you've got!"

The harpooneer sank another one into the whale's back.

Shocked by pain, the whale leaped and thrashed.

Sometimes it got away. Sometimes it turned and attacked.

One blow from its powerful tail, and the lightweight boat would be shattered.

The whale dove deep.

Whiz! Whiz! Both harpoons were attached to a long rope, which uncoiled so fast that it hummed and smoked. The rope might have to be cut. If the line ran out, the boat could be pulled under.

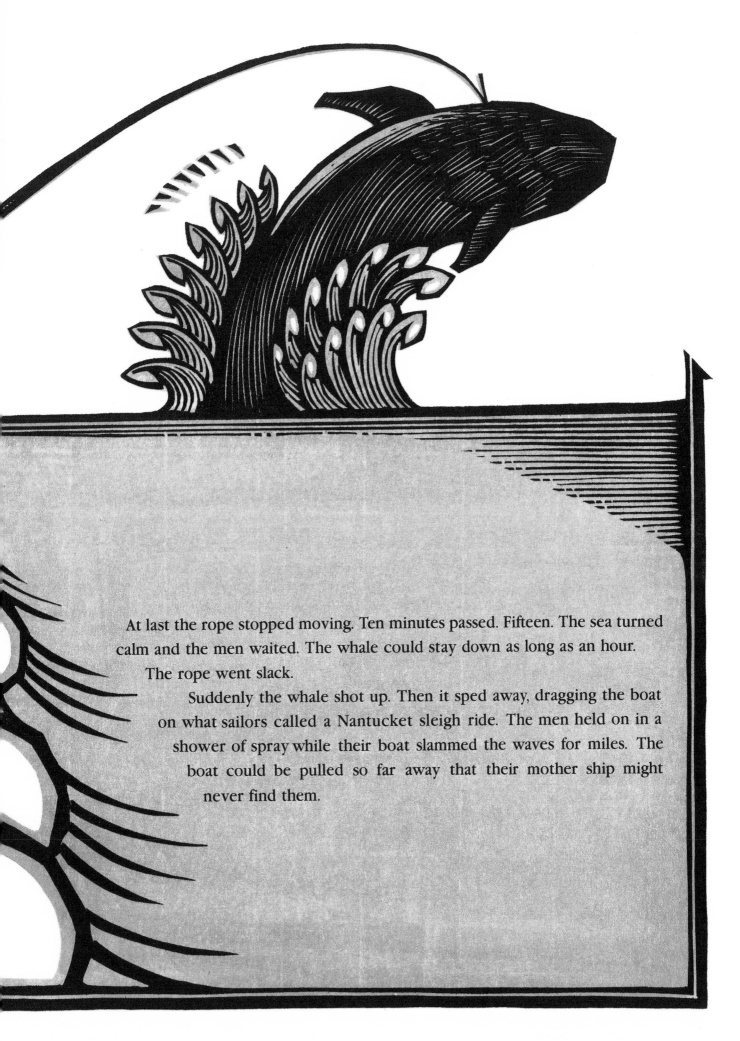

At last the rope stopped moving. Ten minutes passed. Fifteen. The sea turned calm and the men waited. The whale could stay down as long as an hour.

The rope went slack.

Suddenly the whale shot up. Then it sped away, dragging the boat on what sailors called a Nantucket sleigh ride. The men held on in a shower of spray while their boat slammed the waves for miles. The boat could be pulled so far away that their mother ship might never find them.

Finally the whale tired.

"Haul in!" shouted the mate.

The men pulled in the rope, moving the boat closer to the whale.

Now, by tradition, the mate took the harpooneer's place. His lance was razor-sharp. Plunging it into the whale's lungs, he churned it with all his might.

"Cut loose!" he ordered, and the men cut the rope that attached the whale to the boat.

The mist from the whale's blowhole turned pink and then red.

"Stern all!" the mate shouted.

The boat backed clear of the thrashing tail as, mad with pain, the whale beat the sea.

Then the whale went into its final struggle, which whalemen call the flurry. Blood gushed from the creature's blowhole as it swam in furious circles.

A moan rose from deep within the giant.

An hour after the lance had struck, the huge carcass rolled on its side, fin up. The whale was dead.

Now the hard work began. The tired men hauled on their oars to tow the whale back to the ship, where it was chained alongside.

The crew lowered a platform over the whale for the captain and his mates to stand on as they did the cutting-in. They had to work fast before the sharks and the birds stole their catch.

A sperm whale's head would be cut off and hauled onto the deck. Climbing into the case, a cavity in the upper part of the head, a man with a bucket bailed out the spermaceti.

The officers cut long strips of blubber from the whale's body with their sharp cutting spades.

As each strip of blubber was hoisted up, the body of the whale rolled, unpeeling like an orange.

At rare times, the men found a treasure in the whale's intestines—a valuable lump of ambergris. It could be sold to a perfume manufacturer for use as a preservative. The rest of the carcass was set adrift.

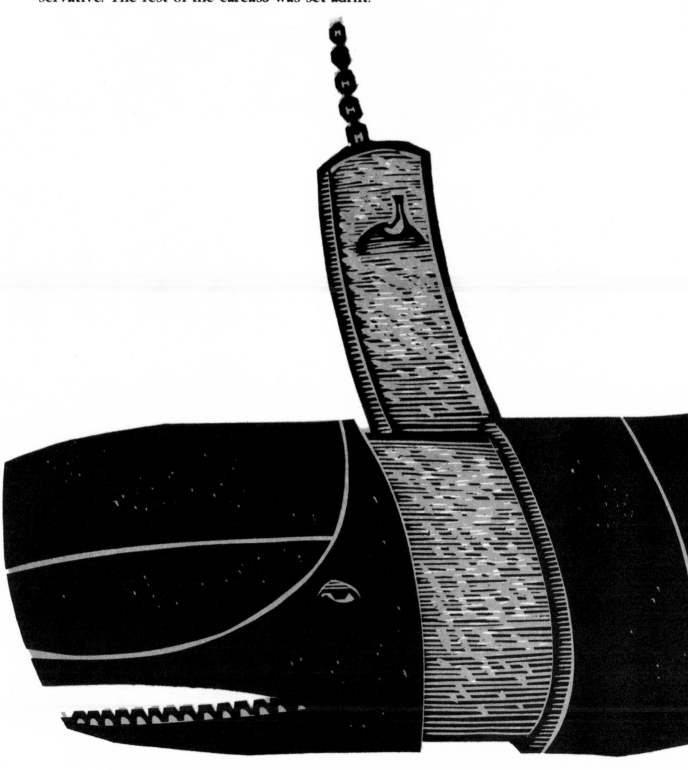

Down in the blubber room, the long strips, called blanket pieces, were cut into foot-square chunks. Then, so they would cook faster, they were sliced into layers like pages in a book.

A sperm whale might take two days to cut up and process. Meanwhile, a fire burned in the brick tryworks on deck as oil was cooked out of the blubber. What remained of the blubber after its oil was cooked out was thrown into the fire as fuel.

30

Smoke rose for hours, blackening the sails. The smell was horrible. After all the oil had been obtained, the decks had to be scrubbed clean of grease and blood and the try-pots had to be polished.

In two days the oil was cool enough to pour into barrels that were then stowed in the hold. The average whale produced 45 barrels. On a successful trip, the whalers might fill 2,400 barrels from as many as seventy whales. Back home, each man received a share of the profits according to his job. When a ship came home with its hold full, it was said to have "greasy luck."

That luck didn't last forever. In 1859, petroleum oil was discovered in Pennsylvania, and it was much cheaper to obtain than whale oil. Because of the scarcity of whales and the rising cost of finding them, investors turned to other industries. By the start of the Civil War in 1861, the important days of American whaling were over.

The industry's decline was hastened when Northern whaling vessels, including almost the entire Arctic fleet, were captured by Confederate ships during the war. Later, fifty-nine more ships were wrecked, trapped in Arctic ice.

The discovery of petroleum oil didn't mean the remaining whales were safe. Although the industry gradually died out in the United States, it was continued by other countries.

Blue whales, the largest animals that ever lived, and finback whales had always been too fast and powerful to catch. Then, in the late 1860s, a Norwegian named Sven Foyn perfected a harpoon cannon that he mounted on a steamboat.

When a harpoon hit, a bomb exploded, killing even a blue or finback whale. No ships were large enough to store all the whale products from these kills, so dead animals were towed to factories on shore. Within just twenty years, blue and finback whales had nearly vanished from northern oceans.

34

In 1904, Carl Larsen, another Norwegian, set up the first whaling station near the Antarctic Circle, the richest whaling grounds in the world. By 1923 he introduced factory ships on which whales killed by diesel-powered boats could be processed in an hour. Now the biggest catches of all time took place. Over 39,000 blue whales and finbacks were killed in the 1939 season alone. As these larger, oil-rich species disappeared, more of the smaller species had to be caught if whalers were to make a profit.

In 1946, in order to preserve the industry, seventeen nations formed the International Whaling Commission to regulate the killing of whales.

Since 1971, all whaling has been prohibited in the United States. Substitutes for whale oil are used in the U.S. to make soap, paint, varnish, cosmetics, margarine, and lubricants for fine machinery. However, whale oil is still used for these purposes in some countries. Whale meat is a popular food in Japan, where there has always been a shortage of red meat. Ground whale meat and bones are also used there as animal feed and fertilizer.

In 1986 the Whaling Commission voted to ban commercial whaling. However, the Commission has no power to force the whaling nations—Japan, Iceland, Norway, and the Soviet Union—to agree to the ban. These nations still want to fish commercially for the less endangered whales, and they are also killing whales for what they call "scientific study."

Now only small numbers of some whale species are left. Other species are

close to extinction. But wherever their dark shapes rise, whales still fascinate humans. Every summer, boatloads of people search the waters off Cape Cod, hoping to catch a glimpse of one.

Organizations such as Greenpeace, U.S.A., and The World Wildlife Federation are working to save the whales that remain. Those of us who care about the fate of the whales can help by joining these groups in their fight.

WHALING TERMS

AMBERGRIS — A rare, waxy substance that forms to protect a sperm whale's intestines from irritating objects. Ambergris is used to preserve the fragrance in perfume.

BALEEN — Triangular horny plates that hang from the upper jaw of certain whales to filter food out of the water.

BLOWHOLE — A nostril on top of a whale's head. The blowhole has flaps that close when the whale dives.

BLUBBER — The layer of fat that lies beneath a whale's skin to keep it warm. In some whales this layer is two feet thick.

BLUE WHALE — The world's largest animal, reaching at least seventy-five tons in weight and ninety feet in length. Because only a small number are left, the blue whale is now a protected species.

BOW — The front of a boat.

CASE — A hollow in the upper half of a sperm whale's head filled with spermaceti. A case may contain as much as fifteen barrels of oil. Scientists think that this oil-filled hollow helps the whale survive the pressure of mile-deep dives.

CROW'S NEST — A small lookout platform nailed to the highest mast.

CUTTING-IN PLATFORM — A narrow plank that hangs from the side of a whaling ship, on which the men can stand when they cut up the whale.

DROGUE — A chunk of wood about two feet square or an inflated skin attached to the harpoon line, which prevents the whale from swimming fast or diving deep.

FIN OR FINBACK WHALE — The second largest whale.

GAM — A visit between the crews of two whaling ships at sea.

HARDTACK — A hard bread or biscuit.

HARPOONEER — The boat-steerer who pulls the forward oar in the boat, harpoons the whale, and then steers while the mate kills it.

HARPOON — A barbed spear used to catch whales.

HOLD — The inside of the boat below the lower deck.

LANCE — A spear used for killing whales.

LOG — A record book of daily life aboard ship.

MATE — An officer on a ship in charge of the deck, crew, and whaleboats.

NANTUCKET SLEIGH RIDE — The whaling term for when a harpooned whale tows a boat behind it while trying to free itself.

RIGHT WHALE — A baleen whale much valued by the early American whalers because it was a good source of oil and whalebone. The right whale was easy to catch since it swam slowly and bred in shallow water. Because it had so much blubber, this whale's carcass floated easily. Now a protected species, the right whale is considered to be the most endangered of the great whales.

SCRIMSHAW — Objects carved and decorated by whalemen from the teeth or lower jawbone of a sperm whale.

SHORE STATIONS — Outposts on land where whales are brought to be processed.

SPERM WHALE — A toothed whale whose blubber made oil of the highest quality. A hollow in its large head contains spermaceti which gives the whale its name.

SPERMACETI — A clear oil found in the head of a sperm whale. Exposed to air, it hardens to a waxy substance prized in making candles.

STERN — The back of a boat.

SPOUT — A jet of warm, moist air exhaled from a whale's blowhole that can be seen as a plume of mist.

TRYING-OUT — The process of cooking whale blubber to remove the oil.

TRY-POT — A large metal pot in which the oil is cooked out of blubber.

TRYWORKS — A brick furnace on the ship's deck that held the try-pots.

SELECTED BIBLIOGRAPHY

(Children's books are indicated by an asterisk [*].)

"The Adventures of a Haunted Whaling Man: A Diary of 1855-58." *American Heritage* 28, no. 5 (August 1977): 46-65.

Allen, Joseph Chase. *Tales and Trails of Martha's Vineyard*. Boston: Little, Brown & Co., 1949.

*Cook, Joseph J., and William Wisner. *Warrior Whale*. New York: Dodd, Mead & Co., 1966.

*Crisp, Frank. *The Adventure of Whaling*. New York: Macmillan, 1954.

de Crèvecoeur, J. Hector St. John. *Letters from an American Farmer*. London: J. M. Dent & Sons Ltd., 1782.

"ECO." Published on the occasion of the 42nd Annual Meeting of the International Whaling Commission, July 1991, by Earth Island Institute and Friends of the Earth.

*Fuller, John. *Whaling World*. New York: Doubleday & Co., 1970.

*Graham, Ada, and Frank Graham. *Whale Watch*. New York: Delacorte, 1978.

"Greenpeace News." *Greenpeace*, July 6, 1990.

"Greenpeace, Ocean Ecology, Japanese Whaling." *Greenpeace*.

*Hough, Henry Beetle. *Great Days of Whaling*. Cambridge, MA: The Riverside Press, 1958.

*McGowen, Tom. *Album of Whales*. Skokie, IL: Rand McNally & Co., 1980.

*Matheu, Martha F. *Whales, Sails, and Scrimshaw*. Reading, MA: Young Scott Books, 1943.

*Meadowcroft, Enid La Monte. *When Nantucket Men Went Whaling*. Champaign, IL: Garrard Publishing Co., 1966.

Phelan, Joseph. *The Whale Hunter*. New York: Time-Life Books, 1969.

*Shapiro, Irwin. *The Story of Yankee Whaling*. New York: American Heritage, 1959.

*Stein, Conrad R. *The Story of the New England Whales*. Chicago: Children's Press, 1982.

Spence, Bill. *Harpooned: The Story of Whaling*. New York: Crescent Books, 1980.

"Whales: Some Species Number Fewer Than Thought, Panel is Told." *Los Angeles Times*, June 13, 1989.

INDEX